# Love to Sew

# Lagom-Style Accessories

# Love to Sew

# Lagom-Style
# Accessories

Debbie von
Grabler-Crozier

Search Press

First published in 2018

Search Press Limited
Wellwood, North Farm Road,
Tunbridge Wells, Kent TN2 3DR

Text copyright © Debbie von Grabler-Crozier, 2018

Photographs by Paul Bricknell (pages 9, 10–17, 22, 26–27, 30, 32, 36, 38, 42, 44, 48–49, 52–53, 56, 58, 62, 64, 68, 70, 74, 76, 79) and styled photographs Stacy Grant (pages 1–7, 19, 21, 23, 25, 29, 33, 35, 39, 41, 45, 47, 51, 55, 59, 61, 65, 67, 71–73, 77–78)

Stitch illustrations by Bess Harding (pages 11–13)

Design copyright © Search Press Ltd., 2018

ISBN: 978-1-78221-607-0

The Publishers and author can accept no responsibility for any consequences arising from the information, advice or instructions given in this publication.

**Suppliers**
If you have difficulty in obtaining any of the materials and equipment mentioned in this book, then please visit the Search Press website for details of suppliers: www.searchpress.com

We invite you to visit the author's blog: sallyandcraftyvamp.blogspot.co.uk

Printed in China through Asia Pacific Offset

*Daisy Pin Cushion, page 18*

*Fika Mug Hug, page 20*

*Dala Horse Hanger, page 28*

*Segling Yacht Shelf Sitter, page 31*

*Gökotta Plant Pot Cover, page 40*

*Dala Elk Cushion, page 43*

*Kära Table Runner, page 60*

*Värma House Shoes, page 63*

# Contents

Hjärta Doorstop, page 22

Hemtrevlig Placemats & Coasters, page 24

Fiska Apron, page 34

Prinsesstårta Bunting, page 37

Träd Tote Bag, page 46

Märkbar Notebook Cover, page 50

Fika Tea Cosy, page 54

Lagnome Wall Hanging, page 57

Söta Äpplen Kitchen Set, page 66

Drömma Hoop Art, page 69

Forelsket Quilted Throw, page 72

Tygkorg Fabric Basket, page 75

# What is Lagom?

I love the concept words which exist in European languages. Great, all-explaining words which say the same to a local that might take half an hour to make clear to anyone else. A few good examples spring to mind, but the word of the day (as far as this book is concerned) is *Lagom*. The word itself comes from Sweden and is all about life in the Goldilocks zone – it means 'just enough' or 'everything in moderation'. Or 'elegant sufficiency', to quote my Nana, who tried to stop me as a child from announcing that I was 'full' after meals. Although it is a Swedish concept, Europe being Europe has meant Lagom has spilled over borders, and now it has cousins living all over the place.

Lagom is about a healthy balance, and the idea of having not too much and not too little is actually something positive to live by. And it is difficult to buy Lagom in the shops: it is a homespun ideology that nourishes using what you have and making do. Now you can see how elegant just one word can be!

To find Lagom and make it part of your life, firstly make it a part of you. Look at your life, accounts, your living space, the garden shed, the way you shop – look at everything and take stock. Is it too much? Too little? How can you change it to better suit you?

The projects in this book are all about injecting little cells of Lagom into your life where they will do the most good. Small things which do the job beautifully and consider you and the world around you. Are you cold? Make a quilt. Not quite warm enough? Consider felt slippers. Is there a small irritation like a door that won't stay put? Make a doorstopp. Notice that I said 'make' and not 'buy'? True Lagom is better made by you and using as much of what you have as possible. In the spirit of this, the projects in this book are all functional and have a very useful purpose. They all fill a need and they all have pared-down features, but with just enough adornment to make you go 'ahhhhh'.

If I had to make one major point about Lagom, it is that it should be personal to you. What I consider personally too much or not enough is irrelevant – my book isn't about an overlord saying 'thou shalt' and 'thou shalt not'. It is about finding what makes you comfortably happy in your own world, so use the instructions inside as a guide to self discovery.

There are twenty projects in this book, and that means twenty areas of your life that can be Lagommed (my apologies to Swedish readers and their horror at this made up word). *Hygge* is the work of a moment – Lagom is a way of life. Focus on the quality of your materials (more about that later) and excessive adornment is not necessary. A bit like life itself really.

Happy sewing!

*Debs*

# Materials & tools

So how do we 'make' Lagom? Sewing is a traditional place to start. Other crafts get a look in too but to keep things simple, this book is all about sewing yourself to moderation. And of course, in keeping with the concept, we only need a few basic bits and pieces to get this thing happening.

## Fabric

Buy the best quality natural fabric that you can. Lagom is about investing in and keeping things of a good standard, and the best fabrics age well. If you choose to use cotton, always but ALWAYS use pure 100 per cent cotton fabric: nylon and polyester or blends will give unpredicted and sometimes awful results.

## Felt

Again, avoid the carnival sideshow spectrum of the acrylic felts. The Lagom story is one of traditional makers who used natural fabrics that they made themselves. Now, while that is not so practical for everyone, purchased handmade wool felt in its lovely muted hues does look the part.

## Thread

Does it do the job? Then it is Lagom. You do not have to spend a month's wages on a spool of thread. Concentrate on the colour and what it brings to the party.

## Interfacing

These are the foundations of your sewing projects and they are not usually things that can be left out. No one likes a sad and droopy bag, or a quilt that feels like a table cloth. This is the one area where I suggest that making do is difficult. Build your collection of sewing materials and equipment gradually, but don't leave these guys out.

## Haberdashery

Zips, elastics, ribbons and that sort of thing are what make a project come together (and stay together too!). Make your item functional, lovely and lasting. Buy less of the best.

## Embellishments

Pared down doesn't mean puritan! You are allowed to have adornments but here again, go for quality and meaning. If you can only have one button choice, make it count.

## Sewing machine

Most of these projects require a sewing machine and I use a Janome Horizon MC 8200 QCP, which I love. It makes me happy just to look at it. But ... I learnt to sew on my Nana's antique Singer, and I have used an elderly Janome for most of my sewing career. Use what makes you happy and what does the job.

## Hand sewing tools

You need the usual suspects: needles, scissors (large for fabric and small for little jobs), a thimble and so on. If something is missing from your kit, that is not Lagom because a left-out gizmo will be a constant irritant. Go find what you need and buy it so that next time, the task at hand will be enjoyable.

## Other special things...

Most of the time, you can make these projects with a very basic kit and everything will go to plan with no stress. However, there are some things that make life a little easier though. Consider these:

**Rotary cutter.** Scissors will do the job, but using a rotary cutter and ruler is faster and more accurate.

**Water-soluble fabric marker.** I could not be without one of these to remind me of essential markings.

**Beeswax.** Really nice for keeping threads untangly.

**Embroidery hoop.** For steering your work in FME (see page 14 for more details on this).

**Bias tape maker.** Makes bias tape making easier and gives you a more professional result (see page 16 for further details).

# Essential hand stitches

Even though most of the projects in this book use a sewing machine, from time to time you need to get a needle and thread out and do some old-fashioned embroidery – think of it as a nod to the traditional techniques of days gone by, when Lagom really was a way of life for everyone.

   The good news is that these stitches are not hard to work, and – with practice – you will come to love this meditative sort of sewing. It is something that can be done anywhere and just about any time.

## Working hand stitches

So why use hoops and thimbles for hand stitching? The truth is that not everyone does. They are not necessary, but they do make your hobby much more pleasant and I find them a great help.

   The hoop keeps the work nicely stretched so that your stitching is perfect. Even when machine sewing, a hoop used upside down will give you something to steer with. It is well worth buying hoops in a couple of sizes if you decide that you like them.

   I have never understood how some people can sew without a thimble! Needles hurt and they will puncture your finger eventually. A well-fitting metal one for the 'driving' finger and a leather thimble for the receiving finger means less injury to your hands – more comfort too, and we are always ready to embrace that!

*Front of the work*

*Back of the work*

# Running stitch

This is one of the easiest stitches of all and it is used a lot in traditional embroidery work. Make sure that you keep an eye on your technique. The trouble with this stitch is that the stitches can get bigger and bigger if you don't watch out. That means unpicking, so it is better to keep stock of what you are doing from the get-go.

Bring the knotted thread up somewhere on the design (A). Instead of going down again as in a straight stitch, go down and up through the fabric a few times (B and C) with a rocking motion and then pull the needle – this way you will get a few running stitches at once. Keep going until you complete your row.

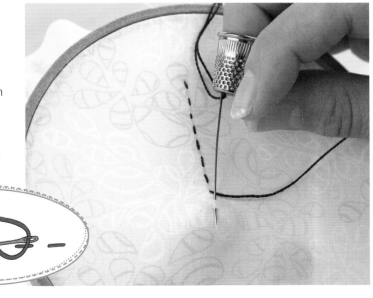

# Back stitch

Back stitch is a great one to learn if you like outlines, text and that sort of thing. Once again, keep it even and if you really have trouble, try marking dots where the stitch should be with your water-soluble marker until your get you eye in.

Begin with your threaded needle and come up from the back of the work (A). Go down at B which, as you can see from the line, is behind A. This is the back bit.

Come back up at point C which is a little ahead of A. C now becomes the new A, and A is the new B. Go back down again at A (through the same hole, so that you get your unbroken line) and go up through the fabric at D.

Continue in this way until you have the line that you want.

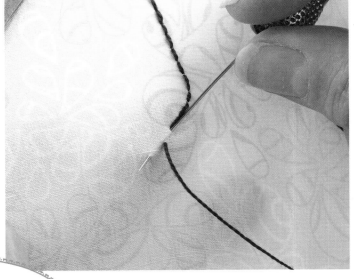

# Cross stitch

This one isn't a proper cross stitch which you do on an evenweave fabric and with a chart. This is a freeform version where you judge where to put the stitch. In some ways it is easier than the 'normal' one, but it can be harder too. The trick here is to keep an eye on what you are doing and don't let the stitches change size or shape. And freeform doesn't mean sloppy! As with the other stitches, make some marks on the fabric first if you are consistently having problems. Your water-soluble marker is your bestie!

Begin with a knotted thread and bring it up where you want to begin the stitch (A). Take it down again at a point diagonally across from where you came up (B).

Bring the needle up at a point below your second stitch (C) and then down diagonally, crossing over the first thread (D). Repeat.

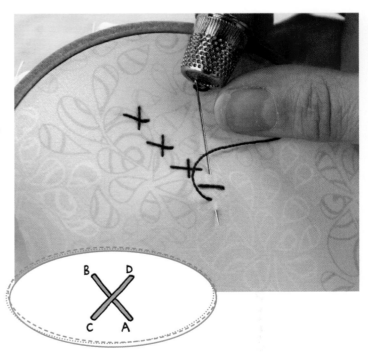

### Tip
The idea here is to make little square boxes with a cross in the middle. If they are slightly off kilter, not to worry – it makes them look more handmade,

# Chain stitch

I really love this one; visually, it is the slightly better, upholstered version of backstitch, and it is also great for text and borders. You will find this one on a bird wing on pages 69 to 71.

Bring the thread up from the back of the work (A), loop the thread around the tip of the needle and hold it in place with a thumb, and then take the needle back near to where you came up, as close as possible to the first point (B).

The needle will be quite flat against the work at this point. Gently pull the needle and thread through point C until the thread is taut but the loop intact. Keep going in a similar way until you have a chain as long as you need.

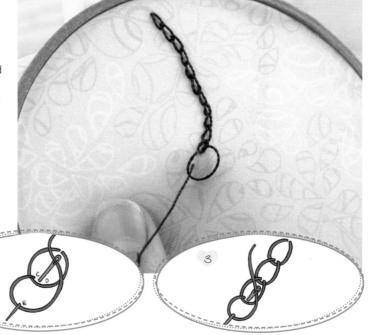

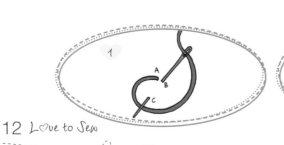

# French knot

This is a classic stitch and although there are many ways of making a French knot, this is one of the easiest. You can make the knot larger by wrapping the thread around the needle a few more times.

Begin by bringing the thread up from the back of the work. Pick up a tiny amount of fabric a few threads away from your starting point. Wrap the thread around the needle about three times. Slide your wraps down the thread to make a knot. Go back down near to where you came up (B), leaving a little knot behind.

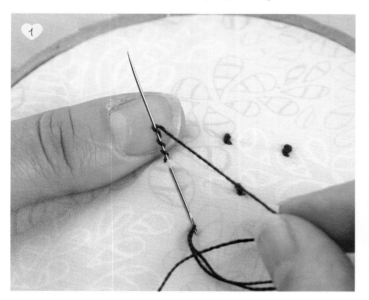
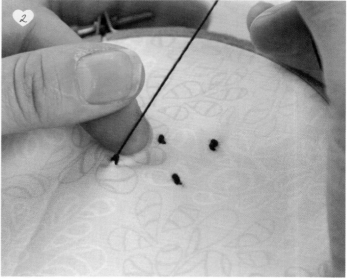

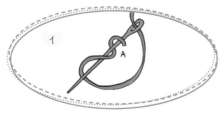
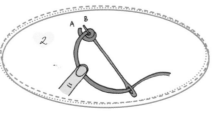
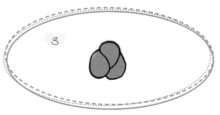

# Basic techniques

## Appliqué

Appliqué is a great way of embellishing your work and telling a story with pictures. There are many types of appliqué but I would like to concentrate on my favourite one. It is my favourite because it is easy, always looks great and I've found it is the best way to use up scraps. In fact, on that last point, start keeping scraps of fabric with appliqué in mind. Zip-lock bags with a different colour in each are a great place to start, and are a nice and attractive way to stay organized.

We call this sort of appliqué 'raggy edged' because we don't need to worry about finishing the edge. Fear not: it will not fray because in free motion embroidery (more about that on the right) the stitches are very close together, which not only stops your design from fraying but means your work can even survive the wash.

What's not to love!

*1* Prepare your shape and glue it in place with a regular glue stick (I like Pritt best) – this means it cannot move about and you don't have pins to get in the way.

*2* Don't fret about being too neat here. Choose an appropriate coloured thread and, coming in from the edge just a bit, sew around the piece. On larger pieces of fabric go around the edge twice, and on smaller ones just once.

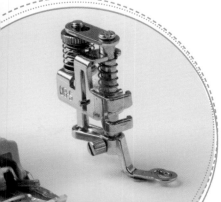

**Darning foot –**
*For free-motion embroidery*

### Free motion machine embroidery

Hand in hand with raggy-edged appliqué is free motion embroidery (or FME). This is a cute technique and can be seen everywhere at the moment. Your machine manual will provide information on how to do it on your particular model but, essentially, you need to either set the stitch length to zero (older models) or drop the feed dogs – this means moving out of the way the little metal plate with teeth under the needle, which is responsible for pulling the fabric through in one direction only. You are then free to manoeuvre in all directions. Harder to explain than it is to do!

Sometimes a pattern will ask for more detail to be sewn on than just around the edge of the piece; in these instances, details will always be provided on the template.

Start with your shape that you want to appliqué – let's do another heart. Glue it down, as instructed above, then hoop up! Simply use an ordinary embroidery hoop upside down to give yourself something to 'steer with'. Attach a darning foot to your sewing machine and, as I touched on in Step 2, come in just a bit from the edge and sew around the piece once or twice.

# Slip pockets

This book is all about Lagom, which means 'just enough' – the slip pocket is the embodiment of this concept. Yes, we can go to town with zips and ties and all sorts of other closures but, actually, the slip pocket just gets the job done without all the fuss, and it is a great place to start if you are new to sewing additional features onto your designs.

I hate opening a beautiful item to find loose threads and raw edges inside. Lining an item is easy, so I am going to show you how to make a lined slip pocket. And it is actually easier than any other kind!

### Tip

Seam allowances are taken into account for all the templates at the back of the book, and are all ½cm (¼in) unless stated otherwise.

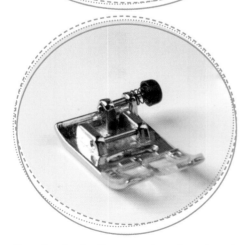

**Regular foot** – *For general sewing; almost all the projects inside use this foot*

1 Begin by cutting the interfacing to size. This will be the size of the finished pocket. Let's say 10cm (4in) sq. Now cut a piece of lining and a piece of outer fabric approx. 2cm (¾in) bigger than the interfacing, and then fuse the interfacing centrally to the wrong side of your chosen outer fabric.

2 Now place the interfaced outer fabric right sides together with the lining and pin. Sew around the very edge of the interfacing, leaving a gap at the bottom for turning inside out.

3 Trim the seam allowance back to 'normal' – this is ½cm (¼in) – and then cut across the corners to reduce bulk. Be careful not to snip into the stitched lines.

4 Turn out through the gap and then press so that the edges are perfect. The pocket is now ready to use, and will be topstitched on with a coordinating thread.

# Free wave motion quilting

As I am sure you will know, there are lots of ways to quilt something. Again, let's make this easier on ourselves and just stick to one technique. This is my trademark quilting technique, and I thought that you might like to learn this one.

It is a wave pattern that is entirely random; not only is this much easier to sew on your machine, it also means that no one can look at your quilt and say that the stitching is wrong! Use it on anything that you need to quilt. I have used this single pattern for all of the quilted objects in this book so you can see how versatile it really is.

Right, here we go!

**Walking foot** –
*For quilting projects and designs that have thick, multiple layers*

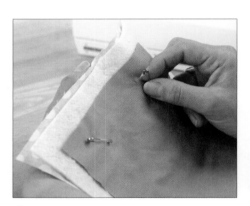

1  Make your 'sandwich', which means placing your backing and wadding/ batting face down, and then the top fabric face up. Pin so that no movement is possible.

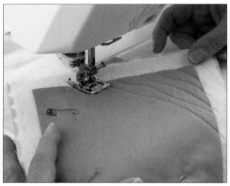

2  Attach a walking foot to your machine and begin quilting with a randomly wavy line. Your walking foot will minimize fabric shift, and just go slowly until you get your bearings. Now come back and make another wavy line going in the other direction.

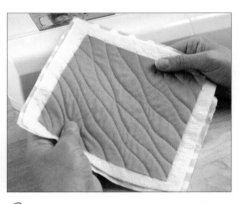

3  Keep going until you have lots of wavy lines. You can use any thread you like; I have used a contrasting one here so that you can see the technique.

## Tip

Always make the wadding/batting and the backing slightly larger than your main fabric, because the three layers will move around and creep (thank you physics) and it can be a disaster. You won't always need to apply backing: the Dala Elk Cushion (page 43) and the oven mitts in the Söta Äpplen Kitchen Set (page 66) don't have any backing, for instance, but the quilting technique is the same.

# Bias binding

Raw edges on your designs are not always appealing and sometimes, on quilts for example, the raw edge is trimmed and then bound with bias binding. Bias is different from straight binding in that it is cut diagonally instead of on the straight grain of the fabric.

My trademark quilt corner is rounded instead of mitred and this looks nice as well as being easier. But it must have bias binding to avoid puckering on the curve.

You can buy bias binding in your local sewing shop or any online stockist, but you are limited to the manufacturers' colours. The good news is that it is easy to make bias binding yourself. Let me show you how…

1  Begin by cutting strips out of your fabric on the bias (forty-five degree angle to the selvage edge of the fabric). The strips need to be about 3.5cm (1⅜in) wide, and as long as you can get out of your fabric.

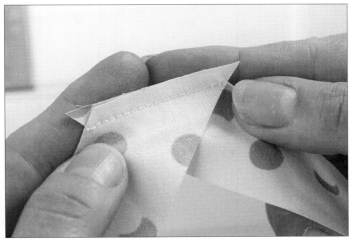

2  Join the strips by placing right sides together at a right angle, and lining up the raw edges. Notice the little 'ears' that are hanging over? This ensures that, when the strip is opened out, it will be straight.

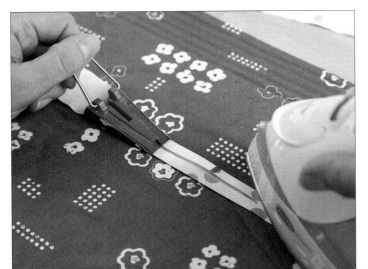

3  Fold in half lengthways with the right sides out and press. If you are applying the tape by sewing machine, you only need this first fold. Otherwise, fold the two raw edges in towards the centre, fold and press again. You can use a bias tape maker to make this easier.

## Template

*(For full-size template, see Pattern Sheet A)*

### Tip

You need only glue the centres of the daisies, as this is simply to anchor the flower shape to the fabric. The stitching in Step 3 then secures the flowers on your cushion.

# Daisy Pin Cushion

Pincushions are handy and this one has the added virtue of being easy to make, too. It is a great place to start if you are a beginner.

Did you know that if you fill your pincushion with un-soaped, fine steel wool it will sharpen your pins every time you push them in or pull them out? It is a great tip for keeping them nice and ready for use.

## Materials

- ♥ 2 pieces of wool felt in light blue and white, each measuring 22.5 x 55cm (11 x 18in/fat eighth)
- ♥ 10cm (4in) sq. of wool felt, yellow
- ♥ polyester stuffing/fiberfill (such as Deco-Wadding, Vlieseline)
- ♥ coordinating threads

## Tools

- ♥ your usual sewing needs
- ♥ glue stick

1   To begin with cut two 12.5cm (5in) squares from the blue felt; also cut two daisies and two centres from white and yellow felt, using the template.

2   Take one square of blue felt and glue your first daisy shape (petals then the centre) into the middle.

3   Using white thread, attach the white flower shape by stitching lines right down the middle of the petals. Lay the second daisy over the top, staggering the petals and also sewing right down the middle of each petal. Leave the daisy petals loose on both sides of the sewing line for a 3D effect.

4   Swap to the yellow thread and sew the remaining centre onto the flower.

5   Take the other felt square and, with the right sides together, sew around the perimeter, leaving a gap for turning out. Cut across the corners to reduce bulk and turn out through the gap. Stuff the pincushion well with stuffing/fiberfill and close the gap.

## Template

*(For full-size template, see Pattern Sheet A)*

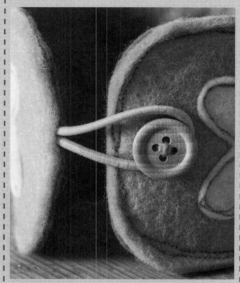

# Fika Mug Hug

*Fika* is one of those almost untranslatable words from Sweden. It actually refers to a coffee break, usually accompanied by beautifully homemade cakes and pastries. And you cannot fika alone! Company is important so put down your tools, put the kettle on and take this seriously – oh, and make some mug hugs for you and your little fika group. The mood is important!

## Materials

♥ piece of thick beige wool felt for the outer, measuring 22.5 x 55cm (11 x 18in/fat eighth)
♥ 4 pieces of thin wool felt in three shades of pink for the lining and hearts, measuring 22.5 x 55cm (11 x 18in/fat eighth)
♥ 10cm (4in) of round elastic in appropriate colour
♥ 1 cute button (such as medium-sized wooden one)
♥ thread, pink

## Tools

♥ your usual sewing needs, inc. darning foot for FME
♥ glue stick
♥ embroidery hoop for FME (optional)

1 Firstly, measure your mug. This project has no pattern as such and this means that you can custom fit it very easily for any mug. Measure your mug around the 'waist' – mine is 28cm (11in) in circumference. Subtract 1cm (⅜in) from this. Now measure the height – mine is 10cm (4in). Subtract 2cm (¾in). This means that the size I need to cut my felt pieces is 27cm (10⅝in) x 8cm (¼in). Cut two felt panels at this size, using the thick and one of the thin pieces of felt. Find a small, round household object to lay your felt on and use this to help you cut round corners for the two pieces. Put the thinner one aside for the lining.

2 Using the heart template, cut out six hearts from your selection of pink felt. You need to cut two of each colour. Position the hearts down the middle of the outer felt panel with their tails pointing towards the centre. Start at the centre, beginning with the two dark hearts, followed by the two medium and two light. Glue them in place.

3 Set your machine up for FME and embroider the hearts with the pink thread. Lightly glue the embroidered outer to the lining piece. Fold the elastic over to make a loop and tuck it in between the lining and outer pieces at the shorter ends.

4 Embroider around the outside of the two panels to attach them to one another, and to secure the elastic loop. Trim all threads away, and sew the button onto the short end of the mug hug on the opposite side to the loop. Put the kettle on!

**Tip**

If you'd like to make a set of mug hugs, consider making each one in different colours, to have a carefully mismatched set where the design is the unifying quality.

## Template

*(For full-size template, see Pattern Sheet A)*

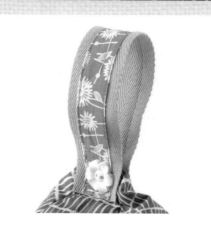

# Hjärta Doorstop

Practical and pretty is the motto here. No one likes a door that won't stay put, especially when there is a warm summer breeze waltzing through the house. The ubiquitous heart shows its face again. This is a much loved folk emblem and always nice to see.

Swap the gravel for dried beans if you like; this little doorstop will still do the job for you.

## Materials

- piece of stripy grey-white print fabric for the sides, 35cm (14in) sq.
- piece of pink floral print fabric for the base, measuring 22.5 x 55cm (11 x 18in/ fat eighth)
- piece of lime green wool felt, 10cm (4in) sq.
- piece of light-weight fusible wadding/batting (such as H630, Vlieseline), measuring 35cm (14in) sq.
- 25 x 3.75cm (10 x 1½in) of lime green cotton tape
- coordinating thread
- 2 flower-shaped buttons
- gravel or dried beans

## Tools

- your usual sewing needs, inc. darning foot for FME
- glue stick
- scalloped pinking shears
- embroidery hoop for FME (optional)

1 Make 25cm (10in) straight binding from the pink fabric. Cut a piece 25cm (12in) long and 4cm (1½in) wide. Fold the two outer raw edges in by ½cm (¼in) on both sides and press. Sew the straight binding to the centre of the cotton tape with coordinating thread.

2 Using the triangle template and the grey fabric, cut four triangles and interface them with the iron-on fusible wadding/batting. With the pink fabric, cut a base measuring 23.5cm (9¼in) sq. and interface that too.

3 Using the large, medium and small templates cut four hearts, two from green felt and two from the pink fabric. Layer the green felt hearts under the pink ones, and then place the heart pairs onto one of the interfaced triangles. The larger heart goes on the bottom. Attach the hearts using FME, making sure they are well in from the sides to allow for seam allowance.

4 Sew the four grey triangles together to make a pyramid. Add the base, sewing right around the edge and leaving a gap for turning.

5 Turn out through the gap and gently manipulate the corners of your pyramid so that they are sharp. Attach the prepared tape to the apex of the pyramid and sew the buttons on the front and back.

6 Fill with gravel or beans, and then hand sew up the gap in the base.

## Template

*(For full-size template, see Pattern Sheet B)*

### Tip

This is a handy trick
when sewing two pieces
of fabric together: instead of
having both the same size, make the
backing a little larger than the fabric
and then trim it back when you have
sewn the edge. It only needs to
be about 1cm (⅜in) larger all
around to make
this work.

# Hemtrevlig Placemats & Coasters

Summer houses are popular in Sweden and it is estimated that around half the population escape to their beloved little wooden huts on the shores of any of Sweden's 100,000 odd lakes! But these little cabins are not just sheds. Oh no. They are *Hemtrevlig* (homely) and they have just enough of the right comforts. Fun fact: Did you know that Abba used a summer house as a place to compose favourites such as 'Fernando' and 'Dancing Queen'?

Bring a little tranquillity and homeliness to your dinner table with some matching placemats and coasters. Nothing says Lagom like laying the table with a set like this.

## Materials

- ♥ length of denim fabric, 1m (40in)
- ♥ length of backing fabric, 1m (40in)
- ♥ piece of white solid quilting cotton, measuring 45.5 x 56cm (18 x 22in/ fat quarter)
- ♥ piece of red blender fabric, measuring 45.5 x 56cm (18 x 22in/fat quarter)
- ♥ piece of light-weight fusible wadding/ batting (such as H630, Vlieseline), 50cm (20in) sq.
- ♥ white thread and red thread for FME
- ♥ coordinating blue thread for quilting

## Tools

- ♥ your usual sewing needs, inc. darning foot for FME and a walking foot for quilting
- ♥ glue stick
- ♥ water-soluble marker
- ♥ embroidery hoop for FME (optional)

1  Begin by cutting the denim. You will need four placemat-sized pieces from it, measuring 33 x 49cm (13 x 19¼in). Interface the denim on the wrong side with a piece of wadding/batting the same size. In addition, cut four placemat backing pieces, each slightly larger than the denim. Use this same principle to cut four coasters too: the denim and wadding/batting is 15cm (6in) sq. and the backing is a little larger.

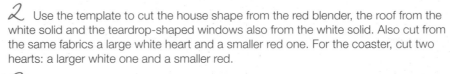

2  Use the template to cut the house shape from the red blender, the roof from the white solid and the teardrop-shaped windows also from the white solid. Also cut from the same fabrics a large white heart and a smaller red one. For the coaster, cut two hearts: a larger white one and a smaller red.

3  Glue the shapes into place with the glue stick. For the placemat, the house goes in the bottom right-hand corner, 5cm (2½in) in from both edges to allow for the seams. The hearts go under the eaves and the two teardrop-shaped windows under the hearts. For the coasters, place the two hearts on top of one another and place them in the middle.

4  FME the shapes with the white and red threads. Trim them and then swap to a regular sewing foot and blue thread. Take a placemat top piece and pin it right sides together with a piece of backing. Sew all the way around the perimeter, leaving a turning gap.

### Tip

The FME guidelines are easy for this one – use the red thread on the white pieces and the white thread on the red pieces. This sounds like a lot of threading and re-threading but it is worth it. Save time and make one particular colour all at once, production line style.

5  Trim the backing, clip across the corners and turn out through the gap. Switch to your walking foot and channel quilt the mat by sewing five concentric rectangles, beginning right on the edge (this will close the turning gap) and working into the middle of the mat. Allow about 1cm (⅜in) gap between each row. For the coasters, quilt two concentric squares.

6  Repeat Step 5 for the remaining mats and coasters.

## Template

*(For full-size template, see Pattern Sheet B)*

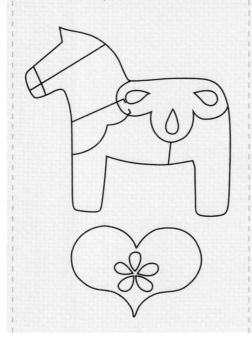

# Dala Horse Hanger

The Dala horse is an important Swedish icon. It originated in Dalarna in central Sweden, and although it started out as a hand-carved toy for children, it has achieved the coveted status as a symbol for Sweden. It certainly is hard to see one and NOT think of Sweden!

Our wall hanging is a celebration of the Dala horse, but let's make it in felt so that we don't have to get the wood carving tools out.

## Materials

- piece of red wool felt, measuring 22.5 x 55cm (11 x 18in/fat eighth)
- piece of white wool felt, measuring 22.5 x 55cm (11 x 18in/fat eighth)
- piece of blue wool felt, measuring 22.5 x 55cm (11 x 18in/fat eighth)
- polyester toy stuffing
- few interesting beads – think plain, unfinished wooden and brightly coloured glass or wood. Include a yellow one for the flower centre
- coordinating thread
- strong thread
- perle no. 8 cotton embroidery thread/floss, red
- large plain silver hoop to hang decoration
- black and white baker's string/twine for the saddle girth and bridle

## Tools

- your usual sewing needs
- fabric glue

1  Using the template, begin by cutting the necessary shapes for the Dala horse. With the red felt, cut out the main body, three teardrop shapes and a square measuring 23cm (9in) sq. Put this latter square to the side for now; you will use this later for backing the horse. With the white felt, cut out the saddle for your horse.

2  Glue the saddle and the accessories onto the horse: the teardrops onto the saddle and the saddle onto the body of the horse. The thinner bridle and the girth on the saddle are made from baker's twine; glue these onto the head and hand sew a couple of anchoring stitches from the back to help keep them in place.

3  With the red perle cotton thread, embroider around the edges of the saddle with a running stitch. The small teardrops can be left bare.

**Tip**

Don't over-stuff the heart and the horse. Just a little is needed to give it some shape.

4  Lay the embellished horse onto the untrimmed red square and pin. Machine sew around the edge with white thread, leaving a small gap somewhere inconspicuous. Stuff the horse shape with polyester stuffing and then close the gap. Trim the felt on the back of the horse.

5  Using the template once more, cut out the shapes needed for the hanging heart. Cut out the heart shape and a 15cm (6in) square for the backing using the blue felt, and then the individual petals for the daisy using the white felt.

6  Make the heart in the same way as the horse, using Steps 3 and 4 as a guide. Glue the white petals onto the heart, and then attach the yellow bead to the centre. Finish the heart in the same way as you did for the horse.

7  Thread a needle with a long length of the strong thread and attach it to the top of the heart. Thread your beads onto it in a pleasing pattern and then anchor the other end to the bottom middle of the horse's belly.

8  Thread up again and, this time, anchor the thread in the middle of the horse's back. Add beads again, and finish with your silver hanging hoop at the top.

**Tip**

When you do the top beaded thread, check to see that the horse is balanced. Simply hold it up by the thread and if it tips to the side, alter the thread position.

## Template

*(For full-size template, see Pattern Sheet A)*

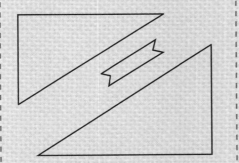

# Segling Yacht Shelf Sitter

Sweden has some beautiful lakes and waterways, and so yachts are not an uncommon sight – any outdoor sport is embraced and sailing (*segling*) is right up there with the best!

This little yacht is a reminder of midsummers on a lake surrounded by beauty. Make it from found wood – normal or driftwood – and a pretty piece of fabric for a sail and a flag. Bliss.

## Materials

- piece of pretty blue and white fabric, measuring 22.5 x 55cm (11 x 18in/ fat eighth)
- tiny scrap of fabric for the sail
- piece of wood approx. 25cm (10in) long – long and thin is best, and driftwood works well
- sturdy stick approx. 40cm (15¾in) long – I like willow for this. It needs to be about as thick as the average little finger
- perle no. 8 cotton embroidery thread/floss, red
- 2 cute heart-shaped buttons – this is a great time to use odd buttons that are just too pretty to throw away

## Tools

- your usual sewing needs
- wood glue
- glue stick
- 2 small eyelet hooks
- drill with wood bit or bradawl

1   Use the template to cut two pieces of main sail and two pieces of the smaller sail. Choose which sail to work on first then place the two pieces right sides together and sew around the perimeter, leaving a turning gap. Turn out through the gap and press it closed. Topstitch around the sail (this will close the gap too).

2   Repeat this process for the other sail. Sew the two buttons into the bottom-left corner of the larger sail.

3   Use the template to cut the small flag from a pretty fabric.

4   Using a drill or bradawl, make a small hole in the middle of the larger piece of wood about the size of the stick, and glue the stick into this – this will become the mast. Use the red perle cotton thread/floss to attach the larger sail to the top and bottom of the mast; do the same with the smaller sail. Take care not to take the sails quite to the top of the mast, as there needs to be some room for the flag at the top, and make them level at the bottom.

5   Stretch the sails – the large one to the front of the hull and the smaller one to the back. Mark where the bottom tip of each sail comes to on the wooden hull and insert an eyelet hook there. Make it slightly further away than the fully stretched sail so that there is a nice amount of tension on the sails.

6   Use the glue stick to coat the flag and fold it around the top of the mast, aligning both sides of it perfectly. Allow this to dry and trim if necessary. Use the red thread/floss again to secure the sail tips to the eye hooks.

## Template

*(For full-size template, see Pattern Sheet A)*

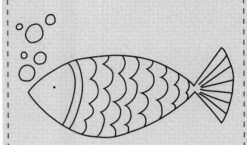

### Tip

The ties for the apron can be as long as you need. Mine are designed for an 'average' person, but you can make them really long to wrap around to the front and tie or just do the usual thing and tie them at the back. Remember, though, that if you make them a longer you may need more fabric. It is fine to join the fabric if necessary.

# Fiska Apron

A handy apron with nice big pockets is needed in every home. The image of the fish (*fiska*) is very important in the coastal areas of Sweden, where seafood is both a major and relied upon staple and export.

As the herring in particular is a major fishy player, it is what I have chosen to star on this apron. A glimmer of silver thread for the embroidery makes this everyday thing more special.

## Materials

- ♥ piece of denim fabric, measuring 40cm (15¾in) x width of fabric (WOF)
- ♥ piece of blue and white print fabric, measuring 70cm (27½in) sq.
- ♥ piece of light-weight, fusible wadding/batting (such as H630, Vlieseline), measuring 45.5 x 56cm (18 x 22in/fat quarter)
- ♥ piece of woven medium-weight, iron-on fusible interfacing (such as G740, Vlieseline), measuring 45.5 x 56cm (18 x 22in/fat quarter)
- ♥ coordinating threads
- ♥ machine embroidery thread, silver

## Tools

- ♥ your usual sewing needs, inc. a darning foot for FME
- ♥ glue stick
- ♥ water-soluble fabric marker
- ♥ embroidery hoop for FME (optional)

### Apron ties

1 Cut two pieces of denim fabric, each 80 x 10cm (31½ x 4in) in size.

2 Fold the denim fabric in half, right sides together, and sew the long side and one short end. Turn the right way out and press so that the edges are perfect. Topstitch the remaining short end with coordinating thread. Repeat for the other tie.

### Front pockets

3 Begin by cutting a piece of denim measuring 49 x 26cm (19¼ x 10¼in) and a piece of the light-weight wadding/batting slightly bigger than this. Fuse it onto the wrong side of the denim fabric and trim back. Cut a piece of the print fabric the same size as the denim – this will be the lining for the pockets.

4 Using the template, cut out a fish from the print fabric and glue it onto the denim piece.

5 Set up your machine for FME and embroider the fish with the silver thread. Embroider on the bubbles too.

6 Snip the thread ends and then, with the right sides together, sew the appliquéd denim front pocket to the print fabric lining; sew along the top edge only, and then flip the pieces over and topstitch the top edge.

## Assembling the apron

7 Cut out two rectangles from the print fabric, each measuring 49 x 38cm (19¼ x 15in) – one of these will be for the lining. Cut a piece of the medium-weight interfacing, making it slightly bigger than your cut rectangles, and iron this onto the wrong side of one of your fabric pieces.

8 Take the trimmed front pocket and lay it onto the interfaced piece of print fabric, carefully aligning the bottom edge and sides. Pin or tack/baste into place.

9 Take the apron ties and pin or tack/baste one on each side of the top of the interfaced print fabric panel, as far as the seam line. Tuck the straps in and poke them into the pocket to keep them out of the way.

10 Lay the lining part of the apron onto the main panel, right sides together, and sew around the perimeter, leaving a gap for turning through around the centre-bottom of the pocket. Turn out through the gap and gently manipulate the apron so that the straps are neat and the corners are perfect.

11 Close the gap with topstitch. The front pocket may gape because of its size, so sew a vertical line down the centre to stop this from happening and to create two handy pockets.

## Template

(For full-size template, see Pattern Sheet B)

# Prinsesstårta Bunting

There is a famous cake in Sweden. It is a half-sphere shape with bright green marzipan and pink roses on the top, and under the marzipan coating are layers of sponge and pastry cream and whipped cream and ... I am drooling on my keyboard now.

It is a big deal anyway and utterly delicious, and called Princess Cake or *Prinsesstårta*. Bunting isn't fattening though, so I think that we should make that instead! This bunting is the perfect way to invite summer into your home. Anyone who knows about Prinsesstårta colours will recognize it at once!

**N.B.** *To simplify things, these amounts are enough to make about five lined bunting flags. If you want more, simply multiply the amounts!*

## Materials

- piece of pretty pink fabric, measuring 45.5 x 56cm (18 x 22in/fat quarter)
- piece of bright green wool felt, measuring 45.5 x 56cm (18 x 22in/fat quarter)
- piece of pretty white ditsy-print fabric for the lining, measuring 45.5 x 56cm (18 x 22in/fat quarter)
- piece of light-weight fusible wadding/batting (such as H630, Vlieseline), measuring 45.5 x 56cm (18 x 22in/fat quarter)
- 14m (55⅛yds) green/white bias binding
- 2 cute buttons for the hanging loops
- 5 small pink satin rosebuds
- coordinating threads for FME and topstitching

## Tools

- your usual sewing needs, inc. a darning foot for FME
- glue stick
- water-soluble fabric marker
- hot-glue gun and glue
- embroidery hoop for FME (optional)

1 Iron the wadding/batting to the wrong side of the pink fabric. Using the template, draw your triangles onto the pink fabric, fitting them in as best you can. Don't cut the flags out just yet, although you may want to trim them into smaller sections – this it to make the FME easier.

2 Cut out felt hearts from the green felt and glue them to the centre tops of the flags, placing them as you see on the template.

3 Using green thread, appliqué the hearts onto the flags and trim back the threads. Cut out the flags.

4 With the right sides together, lay each flag onto a piece of slightly larger lining fabric and sew along the two longer sides. Clip across the bottom point and turn the flag the right way out. Topstitch down each side of the flag and close the top edge with a basting stitch, and then trim so that it is even. Repeat for the other flags.

5 Join the flags together with a few hand stitches (these will be hidden in a minute) and then lay them onto the opened bias binding, butting the trimmed flat edge of the flags up against the middle fold of the bias binding. Fold the binding down to hide the raw edge and then topstitch it right along, closing the binding as you go.

6 Hot glue a rosebud cluster to the centre of each green heart.

7 Fold over the ends of the binding to make a hanging loop and sew on a button to hide the stitching.

**Tip**

A touch of glue from the glue stick will make the binding stay put while you are sewing

## Template

*(For full-size template, see Pattern Sheet A)*

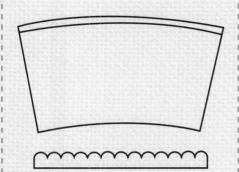

### Tip

On the template there is a line ½cm (¼in) down from the top; this is the grey felt cutting line. When you have cut out the shape, pink along this line with scalloped pinking shears.

### Tip

You can use a water-soluble marker to mark the scallops on the red felt. They do not have to be even – hand drawn is the point!

# Gökotta Plant Pot Cover

*Gökotta* means to get up early to listen to the birds and appreciate nature. This little birdie will wait for you every day and bring the charm and wonder of nature indoors. Perfect for dressing up a pot in need of a makeover, birds have their origins in folk tradition and the use of wool felt makes this project a quick and easy make.

***N.B.*** *This project is designed for a 16cm (6½in) diameter pot with straight sides.*

## Materials

- ♥ 3 pieces of wool felt in cream, blue and dark red, measuring 22.5 x 55cm (11 x 18in/fat eighth)
- ♥ piece of green wool felt, 10cm (4in) sq.
- ♥ black and white baker's string/twine
- ♥ 2 medium-sized plain beachwood beads
- ♥ 1 small black bead
- ♥ coordinating threads for FME and topstitching

## Tools

- ♥ your usual sewing needs, inc. darning foot for FME
- ♥ glue stick
- ♥ scalloped pinking shears
- ♥ embroidery hoop for FME (optional)

1   Using the template, cut two large pieces from the felt, one from the cream and one from the blue. Taking the blue piece (which will become the lining later), place the two short ends together and sew a back seam. Trim the threads and put aside until needed.

2   Using the template once more, cut out the other pieces for the cover: the bird with the rest of the blue felt, the scalloped trim from the dark red felt (measuring 3cm (1½in) high and 46cm (18⅛in) long) and the leaf wing from the green. Glue them into position in the centre of the cream panel.

3 Cut two pieces of baker's string/twine, measuring approx. 8cm (3¼in) long, and tie a knot in the end of both. Thread a beechwood bead onto each piece, and then tuck them up under the bird as marked on the template. You may need to trim the length. Lightly hand stitch these in place, as you will secure them later when you use the sewing machine.

4 Set your machine up for FME and embroider the shapes on with black thread, going around them at least twice. You do not need to be obsessive about neatness. Trim the threads.

5 Sew the small black bead onto the head of the bird to make an eye. As you did for the large blue panel, place the two short ends of your embroidered cream outer piece together and sew the back seam.

6 With the blue lining inside out and the cream outer piece the right way out, slip the cream outer over the blue lining and nest the back seams together so that they are flat. With coordinating threads, sew the layers together and go over the top and bottom a couple of times to secure. If you wish, trim the felt to neaten the edges.

# Dala Elk Cushion

Here we have a little twist on a much loved Scandinavian favourite: the lolloping elk! You can see this image again and again on Scandi designs, and it brings to mind the Swedish forests – those who have travelled through Sweden will often have a black elk silhouette sticker for their car or campervan.

The Dala horse is pretty big up north too, so I have combined the two images to make a special Dala elk cushion. Perfect!

**N.B.** *This project uses my favourite (and signature) free wave motion quilting technique. It is almost impossible to get wrong, even on a large quilt, and you can just let it meander naturally. Try it and be instantly converted!*

## Materials

- ♥ piece of denim fabric, measuring 45.5 x 56cm (18 x 22in/fat quarter)
- ♥ piece of white patterned fabric, measuring 45.5 x 56cm (18 x 22in/fat quarter)
- ♥ piece of red wool felt, measuring 45.5 x 56cm (18 x 22in/fat quarter
- ♥ piece of soft cotton mix, light-weight wadding/batting (such as 279 cotton mix 80/20, Vlieseline), 50cm (20in) sq.
- ♥ cushion insert, 50cm (20in) sq.
- ♥ coordinating thread for quilting
- ♥ perle no. 8 cotton embroidery thread/floss, white

## Tools

- ♥ your usual sewing needs
- ♥ glue stick

1 Begin by cutting out the necessary shapes: a piece of denim and a piece of patterned fabric measuring 50cm (20in) sq., two pieces of cotton mix wadding/batting slightly larger than the denim and patterned fabric squares, and the elk image from felt using the template. Put the elk aside for now.

2 Lay the outer fabric onto the slightly larger wadding/batting and pin. Using a coordinating thread, start to quilt the front and back panels: sew a random wavy pattern onto both the denim and white patterned fabric, working in a diagonal direction. When you have quilted the front and back pieces, trim the wadding/batting to exactly 50cm (20in) sq. and put one aside for the back.

3   Glue the felt elk shape to the centre front of the denim panel. Use the white perle cotton thread/floss to embroider the elk: make a neat running stitch right around the body, including the outline of the elk's head; then, starting underneath the elk's head, hand stitch a row of cross stitches all the way around the body only.

4   Trim the front panel back to 48cm (19in) sq. in size. Leave the back panel untrimmed for now; this will make it easier to sew to the front later.

5   Finally, place the two outer panels together, right sides facing, and sew around the outer edge, leaving a gap for the cushion insert at the bottom. Trim the back panel and clip across the corners to reduce bulk. Turn out through the gap then insert the cushion. Close up the gap with a hidden hand stitch.

**Tip**

The details of where to embroider are on the template. You can use your water-soluble marker to draw them in first. The cross stitches do not have to be perfect but keep an eye on them so that they do not get too wonky!

## Template

*(For full-size template, see Pattern Sheet B)*

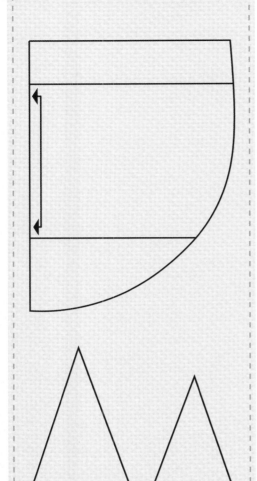

# Träd Tote Bag

Ah woodlands – is it a coincidence, do you think, that the words 'for' and 'rest' come together to make a word about stress relief? No, I don't think so either. I love trees and our forests, so they had to be showcased somewhere.

I love a practical bag, and this one is right up there with the best! Lots of room and some handy pockets – all in all, this tote bag is a walk in the woods!

## Materials

- ♥ **Fabric A:** piece of green patterned fabric for the trees, 40cm (16in) sq.
- ♥ **Fabric B:** piece of patterned neutral fabric for the tree background, 40cm (16in) sq.
- ♥ **Fabric C:** piece of light denim fabric, 50cm (20in) sq.
- ♥ scraps of brown linen for the tree trunks
- ♥ piece of pretty and summery floral fabric for the lining, 1.2m (47¼in) sq.
- ♥ piece of sew-in foam interfacing (such as style-vil smooth foam, Vlieseline), 1.2m (47¼in) sq.
- ♥ piece of soft cotton mix, light-weight wadding/batting (such as 279 cotton mix 80/20, Vlieseline), 1m (40in) sq.
- ♥ packet of 2.5cm (1in) iron-on waistband interlining tape (such as Bundfix)
- ♥ piece of soft, flexible fusible interlining (such as S320, Vlieseline), measuring 45.5 x 56cm (18 x 22in/fat quarter)
- ♥ coordinating threads for topstitching
- ♥ medium-sized silver magnetic clips

## Tools

- ♥ your usual sewing needs, inc. walking foot for quilting

## Front and back

1 Cut two rectangles from Fabric C, one 57 x 7.5cm (22½ x 3in) and one 57 x 13cm (22½ x 5in). Also cut a piece from Fabric B measuring 57 x 22cm (22½ x 8¾in). Sew the smaller rectangle of Fabric C to the top of Fabric B and the larger one to the bottom. Press, and then fuse a piece of fusible interfacing to the back. Don't be too fussy about trimming the edges.

2 Lay the template over the top and, matching the seams up with the relevant lines, draw the shape of the bag onto the three rectangular panels. Don't cut it out yet – this is just to give some idea of where the trees will go in the next step.

3 Using the template for the trees (you have a few to choose from, so make your own forest!), cut out the shapes for the trees from the brown linen scraps and Fabric A. Glue them into place on the middle panel. Allow the trees to stagger over the top of the panel to make them more interesting!

*4* Set your machine up for FME and embroider the trees with corresponding threads. Trim these and then roughly cut out the bag shape. Lay the shape over a slightly larger piece of foam interfacing and channel quilt the bottom of Fabric C section only, leaving a 1cm (⅜in) gap between each line. Attach the whole bag to the foam interfacing with a tacking/basting seam. Cut out the bag.

*5* You have finished the front of the bag. Repeat steps 1, 2 and 4 for the back piece.

## Lining

*6* Use the template to cut two pieces of lining from the floral fabric.

*7* Make two slip pockets next, using the instructions on page 15 to guide you. First, cut two pieces of fusible interlining measuring 20 x 15cm (8 x 6in), and then two more pieces of floral fabric and two pieces of Fabric C that are approx. 1cm (⅜in) larger all around than the interfacing piece.

*8* Fuse the interlining to the wrong side of the Fabric C, taking care to centre it well.

*9* Place an interfaced pocket piece together with a piece of lining (right sides together) and pin. Sew around the very edge of the interfacing, leaving a turning gap on the bottom.

*10* Trim the seam allowance back to 'normal' and clip across the corners. Turn out through the gap and press so that the edges are perfect.

*11* The pocket is now ready to be topstitched into position. Place it approx. 9cm (3½in) down from the top edge of the lining, right in the middle, and topstitch it in place. Repeat steps 8 to 11 for the other pocket.

*12* With the right sides together sew up the lining, leaving a turning gap in the bottom.

*13* Cut two pieces of fusible interlining, about 8cm (3¼in) sq., and fuse them to the wrong side of the lining, right in the middle and about 1cm (⅜in) down from the top.

*14* Attach a magnetic clip to each side of the lining, aligning them carefully. They will need to be clear of the top seam and topstitching, so place them about 5cm (2½in) down from the top edge.

### Tip
Pockets can sag a bit, especially if they are larger. Combat this with some vertical seams to divide them into separate compartments. Makes the pocket nice to use too.

## Straps

**15** Cut four 70cm (27½in) long pieces of interlining tape, and four pieces of fabric measuring 70 x 2.5cm (27½ x 1in) – two will use Fabric C and two will use Fabric D. Fuse the tape to the wrong side of these fabric pieces.

**16** Fold the raw edges on all straps in towards the middle, using the perforations on the tape as a guide, and press. Take two of the fabric pieces for the straps (one from each fabric) and lay them together, wrong sides facing. Using a contrasting thread, pin and topstitch along the straps – twice along each edge and once down the middle.

**17** Repeat for the other strap. Trim them so that they are both the same length.

## Putting it all together

**18** Sew the front and the back pieces together, leaving no gaps. Add the handles next, placing them 15cm (6in) in from the outside edges.

**19** With the lining inside out and the bag outer the right way out, slide the lining on over the outer so that the right sides of the fabrics are together. Line up all of the details and pin. Sew around the top edge and turn out through the gap in the bottom of the lining. Close the gap and push the lining down into the bag.

**20** Topstitch twice around the top edge of the bag with coordinating thread.

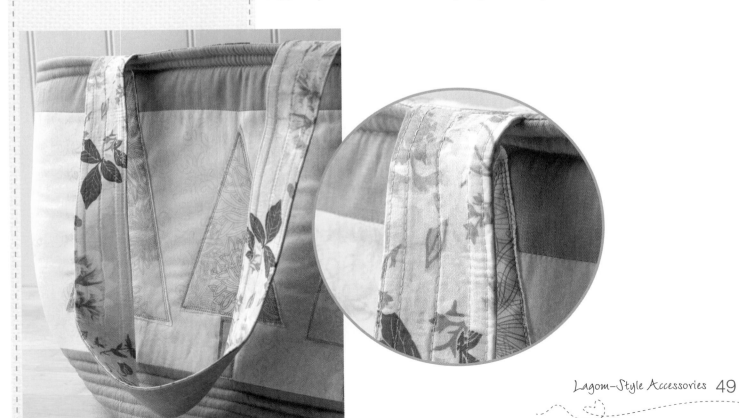

## Template

*(For full-size template, see Pattern Sheet A)*

# Märkbar Notebook Cover

If something is *Märkbar* it is noteworthy and something that you should not pass by. Perfect, then, for a notebook cover!

Whether you use this for an old-fashioned diary, or for something in which to make lists, it is nice to have something pretty and practical just waiting for you to have something to write in it.

**N.B.** *This cover fits a standard A5 notebook with ease.*

## Materials

- piece of denim fabric for the outer cover, 35cm (13¾in) sq.
- piece of text fabric for the lining, 35cm (13¾in) sq.
- piece of pretty coordinating fabric for the slip pockets, measuring 45.5 x 56cm (18 x 22in/fat quarter)
- scraps of green fabric for the appliqué flower and leaves
- piece of medium-weight fusible wadding/batting (such as H630, Vlieseline), 30cm (12in) sq.
- piece of soft, flexible fusible interlining (such as S320, Vlieseline), measuring 45.5 x 56cm (18 x 22in/fat quarter)
- coordinating threads for topstitching
- pink thread for appliqué

## Tools

- your usual sewing needs, inc. darning foot for FME
- glue stick
- embroidery hoop for FME (optional)

1  Cut a panel from your denim fabric, measuring 25 x 37cm (10x 14½in), and interface with the wadding/batting. This is for the main outer cover. Cut two more panels from the denim, measuring 25 x 12cm (10 x 4¾in) and interface these also with the wadding/batting. These form the beginnings of the inner flaps.

2  Use the template to cut out and make the flower from the floral and green fabric scraps. Glue your flower onto the far right of your denim panel, centering the design as best you can. With the pink thread, set up your machine for FME and embroider the flower in place. As you do this, embroider the details too. Neaten the threads at the end. The outer is finished for now, so set this aside.

3  Now for the slip pockets on the inner panels. A slip pocket is very easy to make – use the same principles as for the Träd Tote Bag (see steps 7 to 11 on page 48) but this

time sew only the top seam, flip over, trim, press and then topstitch. The left-hand flap on the inside of the cover will have pockets for pencils. Cut the pocket interfacing from the interlining, measuring 15 x 12cm (6 x 4¾in). Cut a piece of text fabric and a piece from your pretty coordinating fabric, both 1cm (⅜in) larger all around than the interfacing. Fuse the interfacing centrally to the wrong side of the pretty coordinating fabric.

4   With the right sides together, sew the pocket's top seam only. Trim the seam allowances back to ½cm (¼in). The seam allowances on the sides and bottom can be trimmed right back to the interfacing so that the pocket fits over the panel.

5   Flip it all the right way out and press so that the top edge is smooth. Narrowly topstitch along the same edge with coordinating thread.

6   Lay this pocket onto the interfaced denim panel and align the bottom and side edges. Tack/baste the sides and bottom so that all layers are together. Sew three vertical seams down the pocket to create pen holders.

7   Now for the inside of the right flap. Cut two pieces of interlining, one measuring 20 x 12cm (8 x 4¾in) and the other 10 x 12cm (4 x 4¾in). The longer piece will be for the long pocket at the back, and the smaller will be for the smaller front pocket.

8   Cut two pieces of lining and two of coordinating pretty fabric, both slightly larger than the interfacing piece as before (see Step 3), and fuse the wadding/batting to the wrong side of the pretty fabric. With the right sides together, stitch the interfaced pretty fabric to the lining along the top seam only. Trim the seams and flip over, press and topstitch. Align the small and larger pockets' bottom and sides and pin.

9   Lay both onto the denim panel and align the bottom and sides. Tack/baste all the layers together.

10   Take the front panel and the left-hand side flap and, with the right sides together, attach the panel. Repeat with the right-hand side flap.

11   Prepare a piece of lining just slightly larger than the denim outer panel with both the flaps attached. Lay the completed denim outer onto the lining, right sides together, and then pin and sew the perimeter, leaving a turning gap in the middle bottom. Turn out through the gap and press.

12   Fold the flaps in and narrowly topstitch the top and bottom, giving the cover its shape.

### Tip
A very long, deep pocket isn't very practical. Come up from the bottom a little way and sew a seam across to shorten it. Don't go above the front pocket though – this seam looks neater when hidden.

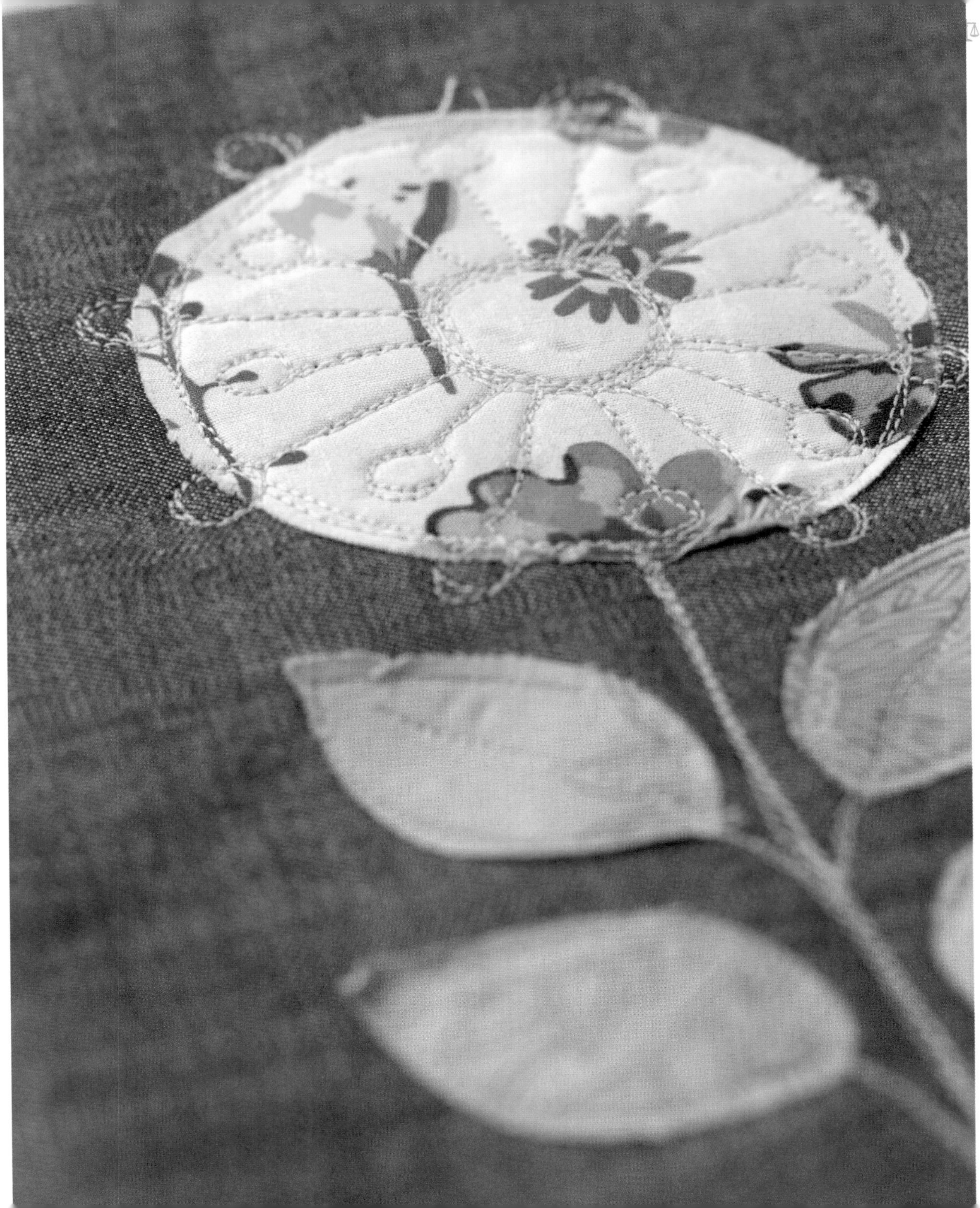

## Template

*(For full-size template, see Pattern Sheet A)*

# Fika Tea Cosy

There is a bit of a mixture in the title of this one! *Fika* refers to a coffee break and it is considered to be very necessary in Sweden. It can be a simple affair just between you and a friend, or it can involve a whole bunch of people. The most important thing is that it is a total pause from the daily tribulations to stop, have a coffee and a pastry or cake. Even the huge corporations in Sweden stop for fika.

So, why the mix up? Well I decided to include our tea drinking friends as well and make a tea cosy! It won't matter that someone is drinking tea instead of the traditional coffee; the important thing is to stop, relax and enjoy. Fika is a ritual and an institution. I promise not to tell the Swedes that someone has smuggled in tea! Shhh...

## Materials

- ♥ piece of plain fabric for the cosy outer, 40cm (15¾in) sq.
- ♥ piece of pretty grey/blue fabric for the lining and allium flower heads, 40cm (15¾in)
- ♥ piece of light-weight fusible wadding/batting (such as H630, Vlieseline), 50cm (20in)
- ♥ faux gold leather bias binding (optional)
- ♥ thread, dark grey
- ♥ coordinating threads for topstitching

## Tools

- ♥ your usual sewing needs, inc. darning foot for FME
- ♥ glue stick
- ♥ water-soluble marker
- ♥ embroidery hoop for FME (optional)

1  Begin by using the template to cut out two outer pieces from the plain fabric and two lining pieces from the patterned fabric. Interface the wrong side of the plain fabric with the wadding/batting and trim.

2  Using the templates, cut three allium head shapes from the grey/blue fabric. You don't need to do this neatly, as they should have a very free-form appearance.

3  Stick them onto the two interfaced outer panels, allowing room for the stems of your flowers – the lowest allium head on mine is approx. 8cm (3¼in) up from the bottom edge. When dry, use the water-soluble marker to draw in the details of the flowers.

4  Thread the machine with grey thread and set up for FME. Embroider the flowers and trim away the thread tails. Mist with water to remove the marker lines.

5  Make the top loop handle by cutting a piece of plain fabric, approx. 20 x 4cm (8 x 1½in) in size. Fold in half lengthways and press. Open out and then fold the raw edges to the centre fold and press. Fold in half again and topstitch along both long sides with coordinating thread. Trim the ends of the loop handle and fold in half shortways to make a loop. Attach to the top of one of the outer panels.

6  I have also added a little gold tag on the side, which you can add as an option. This is just faux leather bias binding and you can find it readily online and in good haberdashers. About 5cm (2.5in) folded over does the trick. Attach to one of the sides of the outer panels.

7  With the right sides together, sew the top curve of the tea cosy outer. Sew the top curve of the lining too, but leave a turning gap somewhere. With the outer the right way out and the lining inside out, pull the lining on over the outer and sew the bottom edge.

8  Turn the tea cosy out through the gap and close it with a hidden hand stitch. Stuff the lining into the outer, but leave a small trim at the bottom (it will look like bias binding but is actually protruding lining). Topstitch around the bottom right on the edge of the trim to keep it in place.

**Tip**
Gravity being gravity, your lining will not stay in the tea cosy when it is upside down! A few stitches inside along the seam line will keep the lining up where it should be.

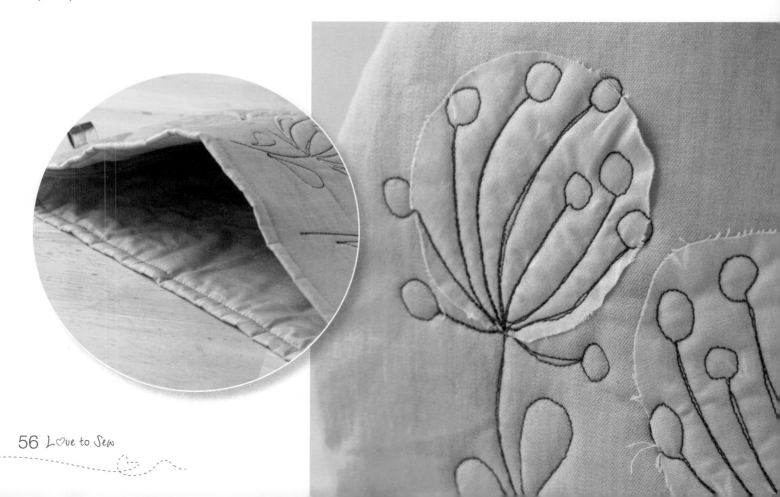

## Template

*(For full-size template, see Pattern Sheet A)*

# Lagnome Wall Hanging

Sweden would not be Sweden without a gnome somewhere! They are an iconic image with much meaning in the north of Europe. In ancient times they have been regarded as both good and bad; in modern times they are protectors for the house, so we are going with that.

This wall hanging embodies the spirit of the *tomte* (gnome) tradition and it even has a Sami tassel on the side, made in sympathetic tradition of these nomadic northern people. Happy days!

## Materials

- piece of muted fabric, 40cm (15¾in) sq.
- 6 pieces of wool felt in red, blue, flesh, peach, grey and black, each 15cm (6in) sq.
- piece of medium-weight fusible wadding/batting (such as H630, Vlieseline), measuring 45.5 x 56cm (18 x 22in/fat quarter)
- coordinating threads, inc. black
- perle no. 8 cotton embroidery thread/floss, olive green
- mustard gold cotton yarn
- black and white baker's string/twine
- small scrap of woven ribbon (such as red and white)
- scrap of long white faux fur, approx. 10cm (4in) sq.

## Tools

- your usual sewing needs, inc. darning foot for FME
- glue stick
- hot-glue gun and glue
- stick or small piece of driftwood, slightly longer than the banner
- embroidery hoop for FME (optional)

1 Begin by using the template to cut a banner shape from the fabric and interface it on the back with the wadding/batting.

2 Cut out and construct the gnome from felt pieces using the template. Use the glue stick to glue the pieces into place on the muted fabric and position as you see it on the template. Cut the beard from white faux fur and hot glue this on. This is the only bit of the appliqué that will not be stitched down.

3 Set your machine up for FME and, with coordinating threads, embroider the gnome and heart onto the front section of the fabric. I have also used some white thread to sew the shine on the toes of his boots. Snip away the thread ends.

**Tip**

These cross stitches are meant to be casual, so don't obsess about neatness. Hand stitched is the look that you are going for and make them slightly larger than usual, at about 1cm (⅜in). Skim through the lining when you are stitching so that they are not visible on the back, rather than going through the full thickness of the fabric and having them come out the back.

*4* Complete the banner by laying the front section over the remaining muted fabric, right sides together. Don't trim the wadding/batting at this stage.

*5* Sew right around the edge of the banner, leaving a gap at the top. Trim the lining, clip the curves and then turn out through the gap. Press the banner and then hand stitch a row of cross stitches along the banner edge with the olive green perle cotton thread/floss. Form a U with your stitches, starting approx. 10cm (4in) from the top. The unstitched part will be folded over to form the casing for the wood.

*6* Fold over the top edge of the banner towards the back so that a casing is formed for the wood. Sew from one end to the other. Push the stick through the casing and make a tie from the baker's string/twine to hang.

*7* Make the tassel by taking a bit of heavy card, about 13cm (6in) long, and winding the yarn around it about thirty times. Tie the top with another piece of the same coloured yarn and cut the bottom. Remove the tassel from the card and then, approx. 2cm (¾in) of the way down, tie the tassel and hot glue a piece of woven ribbon around the tie. Secure the tassel to the left-hand side of the banner.

## Template

*(For full-size template, see Pattern Sheet B)*

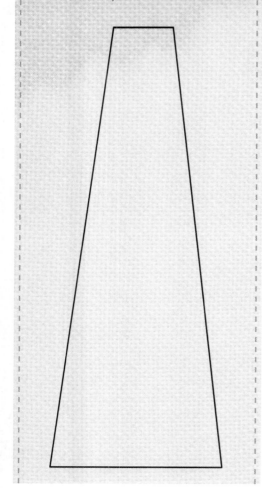

# Kära Table Runner

A table runner is a brilliant compromise between a full and formal table cloth and placemats. It highlights the dining experience and I love the way that it provides a focus down the centre of the table on which you can put candles or flowers and then, during the meal, the plates from which the diners help themselves.

This last point is a great feature of continental European dining – let your guests decide how much food they want. Especially for children, this helps to stop overeating and it makes for a very convivial atmosphere at the table. Try it once – but you will need this runner first!

## Materials

- 5 pieces of various patterned grey fabric, measuring 45.5 x 56cm (18 x 22in/fat quarter)
- 2 pieces of solid grey fabric, measuring 45.5 x 56cm (18 x 22in/fat quarter)
- piece of black and white print fabric for the binding, measuring 45.5 x 56cm (18 x 22in/fat quarter)
- piece of coordinating fabric for the backing, 1.3m (47¼in) sq.
- 1m (40in) of soft cotton mix, light-weight wadding/batting (such as 279 cotton mix 80/20, Vlieseline)
- light grey thread for quilting

## Tools

- your usual sewing needs, inc. a walking foot for quilting
- quilting ruler
- cutting mat
- water-soluble marker
- bias tape maker (optional)
- rotary cutter (optional)

1  Using the template, cut four wedges out of the five patterned and two solid grey fabrics. The best way to do this is to layer the fabric and then place the bottom of the wedge along one side, draw around it with a water-soluble marker and then flip it over and draw the next wedge upside down beside it.

2  You will have some offcuts from your colours. Cut 3.5 x 42cm (1⅜ x 16½in) strips from these.

3   Begin by choosing one strip and a wedge and sewing one to the other. Add another wedge and a strip and then two wedges; of course, make sure that you place the wedges head to tail so that your runner will be straight! Keep going like this until you have a runner that is approx. 2m (2¼yd) long. Trim the end wedges square and press.

**Tip**

Depending on how many strips you incorporate into your runner design, you may have some wedges left over.

4   Cut the backing fabric down the middle and join it to make one long piece, approx. 60 x 110.5cm (24 x 43½in) in size. Press the backing and lay it face down. Cut a piece of wadding/batting the same size and put it on top, and then add your pressed patched panel over that so it is facing up. Pin and then, using the grey thread, quilt over the design with a random wavy pattern. As there are angles in this runner, try and work the quilting across in one direction to avoid any clashes and to unify the design.

5   Trim the three layers even and square up the corners. Using a large tea cup or a similar circular item, round the corners and then bind the runner with the bias binding (see page 15 for instructions on how to make this).

**Tip**

When putting bias binding on by machine, I find it easier to just do the first fold.

## Template

*(For full-size template, see Pattern Sheet B)*

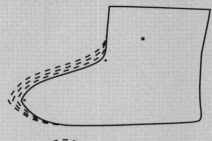

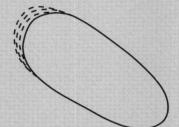

### Tip

You don't need to include the seam allowance when cutting out the two interfacing pieces – they should be 0.5cm (¼in) smaller than the felt so that they will not be visible when you sew together the sole sections.

# Värma House Shoes

It is usual in northern Europe and Scandinavia to take your street shoes off when entering someone's house. Well, when you think about what is on the streets, it is only reasonable! In return, many thoughtful homeowners have a basket of house shoes by the front door for guests to wear. It is an extra nice welcoming touch. These slippers are easy to make from wool felt and they will be appreciated all year round.

**N.B.** *The template for this pattern has included women's UK sizes 4–5, 5–6, 6–7 and 7–8 (EU sizes 37–38, 38–39, 39–40 and 40–41 / US sizes 6–7, 7–8, 8–9 and 9–10 ) for you to use as a guide. For an absolute fit, it is recommended that you measure your foot before cutting out and adjust accordingly.*

## Materials

- ♥ piece of wool felt in green marl, 1m (40in) sq.
- ♥ piece of sew-in foam interfacing (such as style-vil smooth foam, Vlieseline), measuring 45.5 x 56cm (18 x 22in/fat quarter)
- ♥ 2 pretty buttons, red
- ♥ round elastic, red
- ♥ red thread for topstitching

## Tools

- ♥ your usual sewing needs
- ♥ hot-glue gun and glue

1 Using the template, cut eight upper sections from the green felt. Also cut six sole pieces from the felt, including two from the interfacing.

2 Begin with the uppers: take two pieces (these will be the insides of your shoes) and sew the top seam between the dots and the heel seam entirely. Now take two more upper pieces and do the same thing to create the outsides of the shoes.

3 Turn the outers inside out so that the seam is on the inside for both the lining and the outer (it is more comfortable this way too). Pull the outer on over the lining and nest the seams so that they are quite flat.

4 Cut a piece of elastic, about 12cm (4¾in) long, and fold it in half to make a loop. Put this inside the two layers on one front side, about 2cm (¾in) down from the top – you can pin or tack/baste them together if necessary.

5 Thread your machine with red thread and sew the two layers of felt together around the top and the front centre opening, trapping the elastic as you sew. Since the elastic will undergo a fair bit of strain, reverse carefully over the trapped-loop section a couple of times with your sewing machine to secure it well. Sew a button to the upper on the corner opposite to the elastic. The upper is now finished. Repeat this for the other one.

6 Make the soles by laying the outer piece down and hot gluing the foam shape to it, taking care to centre it well. Lay the inner sole piece (lining) on top and tack/baste together to hold them. Place the upper piece over the sole 'sandwich' and pin or tack/baste – I prefer to tack/baste to keep pins out of the way. Sew around the four layers twice with red thread.

**Tip**
You can use a zipper foot to make the sandwich easier to sew, and lengthen your stitch to about 3.5mm (⅛in) to manage the layers.

**Tip**
These house shoes do not actually have a left and right but if you want to create this, place the elastic on opposite sides.

## Template

*(For full-size template, see Pattern Sheet B)*

### Tip

Be very sure to draw the mitt pieces on mirror image! This goes for the lining too when you get to that bit. This is so that they fit together.

# Söta Äpplen Kitchen Set

Sweet apples – surely they belong in every kitchen!

Well, a nice kitchen set does indeed. I love the way that it cheers up the whole room. This is another very practical and pretty way to bring Lagom into your life, and it's speedy to make too. This set will make a beautiful gift that will always be appreciated. Ring the changes with different colours and consider making two mirror image mitts to make oven roast removal even easier.

## Materials

- piece of denim fabric for the outer, 50cm (20in) sq.
- piece of bright red fabric for lining and the apples, 30cm (12in) sq.
- scraps of green fabric for the leaves
- scraps of cream fabric for the apple cores
- piece of grey blender fabric for the trim on the towel and mitt, measuring 45.5 x 56cm (18 x 22in/fat quarter)
- piece of woven medium-weight, iron-on fusible interfacing (such as G740, Vlieseline), measuring 22.5 x 55cm (11 x 18in/fat eighth)
- piece of dense polyester insulated wadding/batting (such as 272 Thermolam, Vlieseline), measuring 45.5 x 56cm (18 x 22in/fat quarter)
- black and white bakers string/twine
- black thread for FME
- coordinating thread for the quilting

## Tools

- your usual sewing needs, inc. darning foot for FME
- glue stick
- water-soluble marker
- embroidery hoop for FME (optional)

### Tea towel

1  Cut a piece from the denim fabric, measuring 46 x 60cm (18⅛ x 23⅝in). For the trim, take the grey blender fabric and mark off an area measuring 46 x 15cm (18⅛ x 6in) – don't cut it out yet. Cut a piece of fusible interfacing the same size and fuse it to the back of the trim. It doesn't matter If it goes over a bit; this is to give the machine something to grab onto while you embroider.

2  Find the centre of the trim line that you drew and then, using the template, cut out the apple pieces and leaves from their corresponding fabric and glue them onto the trim. For the apple, the red fabric is applied first and then the cream goes over it. Draw on the outlines of the seeds with the water-soluble marker.

*3* Set up your machine for FME then embroider on the apple details with black thread. Start with the edges to secure the apples and end with the seeds.

*4* Trim away the threads and then cut out the trim. Mist the trim to remove the marker lines. Fold the two long ends under by ½cm (¼in) and press. Lay the trim onto the towel, 12cm (4¾in) up from one end, and pin.

*5* Swap to the coordinating thread and attach the trim by topstitching close to the edge.

*6* Trim around the towel (especially where the trim overhangs) and hem it. Fold the edges over and then the raw edge under again, taking the trim ends with it. Press.

## Oven mitt

*7* Take two pieces of denim fabric, approx. 30 x 35cm (12 x 13¾in). Using the template and water-soluble marker, draw the mitt shape onto them. Do not cut them out yet.

*8* Cut two pieces of insulated wadding/batting, the same size as the denim, and lay your denim fabric pieces over the top.

*9* For the back: Using a coordinating thread, quilt a random wavy pattern over the mitt. Go slightly over the outer edge of the mitt line. The back is now done and can be cut out.

*10* For the front: Cut out a piece of trim, measuring 6.5 x 20cm (2½ x 8in), and turn the long edges under and press like before. Lay this trim onto the mitt, as shown on the template, and topstitch it on with coordinating thread. This time embroider the apple and leaves straight onto the mitt, as the rough side will be hidden on the mitt and then lined. Cut out the mitt.

*11* Using the mitt template once more, cut out two pieces of scarlet lining.

*12* Cut a piece of baker's string/twine, approx. 25cm (10in) in length, and fold it in half. Attach this as shown on the template to form a hanging loop.

*13* Place the two mitt outers right sides together and sew around the perimeter, leaving the bottom where your hand goes in. Sew around the perimeter of the lining also, making sure to leave a turning gap somewhere on the inside – I find the longest, straightest section of the mitt the best for the turning gap, as it's easier to close later on.

*14* With the outer the right way out and the lining inside out, pull the lining on over the outer. Sew around the top edge and then turn out through the gap. Close up the gap with a hand stitch.

*15* Stuff the lining down into the mitt and topstitch the upper edge with coordinating threads.

## Template

*(For full-size template, see Pattern Sheet A)*

# Drömma Hoop Art

Daydreams are a great way to escape the rat race for a short while each day – flying somewhere on a bird wearing a crown has to be up there with the best!

Remind yourself that a world exists outside your office window with this hoop wall hanging. Hang it near your desk to encourage the occasional flight of fancy, which will no doubt lighten your day.

## Materials

- ♥ piece of neutral, low-volume fabric, 37cm (14½in) sq.
- ♥ scraps of wool felt in blue and green
- ♥ piece of felt for the back, 37cm (14½in) sq. – I have used purple felt to correspond with the thread
- ♥ piece of light-weight fusible wadding/batting (such as H630, Vlieseline), 37cm (14½in) sq.
- ♥ perle no. 8 cotton embroidery thread/floss, plum

## Tools

- ♥ your usual sewing needs
- ♥ embroidery hoop, 25cm (10in) in diameter
- ♥ glue stick
- ♥ hot-glue gun and glue
- ♥ water-soluble marker

1 Begin by taking the neutral fabric destined for the main background and fusing the wadding/batting to the wrong side. Take your embroidery hoop, disassemble it, place the smaller ring on the fabric and draw around it with the water-soluble marker. This gives you your working area.

2 Using the template, cut out the main bird shape with the green felt and its wing with the blue felt. Find the centre of the circle on the fabric and glue on both the green bird and blue wing with the glue stick. Mark the border and the flowers on the bird's head with your water-soluble marker.

## Tip

You can use the actual hoop that you will mount it in to do the embroidery. This is one of the few makes in the book that does not use a sewing machine, so it is perfect for making in a quiet corner whilst sipping pink tea from a pink tea cup (which is what I am doing).

3  Embroider the edge of the bird body with a running stitch and its wing with chain stitch, using the plum perle cotton. Backstitch its crown, adding a French knot on the top of each hair. Work a French knot once more for the bird's eye. Finally, backstitch the border around your bird. Note: for this outer embellishment, go just over the edge of the drawn circle so that the ends are hidden when the hoop is assembled.

4  Fit the embroidery into the hoop and tighten the screw. Lightly mist the front with clean water to remove the marker lines (this will slightly shrink and tighten the embroidery on the hoop too).

5  Trim back excess fabric so that there is about 3.5cm (1⅜in) overhang. Hot glue this to the underside of the back of the hoop to keep it out of the way. Use some interfacing offcuts to fill the back of the hoop so that things stay nice and taut and don't sag. Hot glue the large purple felt piece to the back of your hoop then trim away the excess to create a neat, rounded edge.

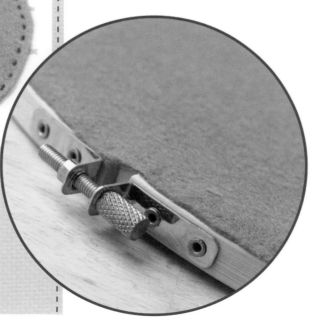

## Materials

- ♥ piece of pink floral fabric, 50cm (20in) sq.
- ♥ piece of white solid fabric, 1m (40in) sq.
- ♥ piece of grey solid fabric, 3.5m (3¾yd) sq.
- ♥ piece of cream patterned fabric for backing, 5m (6yd) sq.
- ♥ packet (or approx. 2.25 x 1.75m/82¾ x 70in sq.) of soft cotton mix, light-weight wadding/batting (such as 279 cotton mix 80/20, Vlieseline)
- ♥ piece of grey bias binding, 5m (6yd) long – this can be homemade or purchased
- ♥ coordinating threads for quilting

## Tools

- ♥ your usual sewing needs, inc. walking foot for quilting
- ♥ quilting ruler
- ♥ cutting mat
- ♥ rotary cutter (optional)
- ♥ bias tape maker (optional)

# Forelsket Quilted Throw

Departing from Sweden for a side trip to Norway, we have the concept of *forelsket*. Once again, there is no comparable term in English that would not take half an hour for a Swede to explain. To put it simply, it means the feeling of first falling in love. How cool is that!

If you have ever needed a cosy hug when you are cold, this is the quilted throw with which to fall in love. Sitting outside on a summer's evening when the chill just enters the air, it is the very thing to wrap yourself and, perhaps, a well-chosen loved one.

### Front of the quilt

1 Begin with the heart border: To make one heart block, cut nine squares of white solid and sixteen squares of pink floral fabric. The squares measure approx. 8cm (3¼in). This block will give a pixilated heart that is very easy to achieve. Start by sewing the blocks together in rows and then join the rows.

**Row 1:** one white, one pink, one white, one pink, one white.

**Rows 2 and 3:** five pink.

**Row 4:** one white, three pink, one white.

**Row 5:** two white, one pink, two white.

Make three more blocks in the same way.

2 Cut the white strips next. They will go between the heart blocks and then the two longer ones will go above and below the hearts. The white strips could be made by cutting multiple squares, but this would take forever and there is no need – when the shapes are quilted, everything will blend in. The strips between the blocks measure 8cm (3¼in) x longest direction of fabric (LOF) available on the straight grain, and the top and bottom strips measure the same. Why use this method? Because it is easy! All you have to do is to worry about the correct width. As long as the fabric is as long as possible, you can simply join the strips in, press and trim – the length will take care of itself.

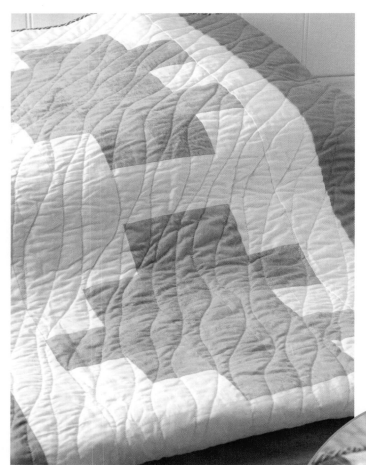

3 Press the heart border and trim it to size.

4 Attach a panel of grey solid fabric to the top of your bordered hearts. This is a whole cloth quilt, so all you have to do is to take the grey fabric, turn it on its side and attach it to the top of the heart row. Trim the excess away.

5 Cut a panel of grey solid, measuring 43cm (17in) x LOF, and attach this to the bottom of the heart strip. Press. The front is now finished.

## Finishing off your quilt

6 Make your quilt 'sandwich' next: Cut the backing fabric in half widthways, and then join down the centre to make a wider piece. Press and lay the fabric face down. The wadding goes next and then the pressed quilt top over that, face up. Pin or tack/baste so no movement is possible.

7 Set up your machine up for quilting and then quilt with a random wavy pattern, working diagonally from one corner to the one opposite.

8 Trim the quilt and square it up. Round the corners (a small plate or saucer is great for this).

9 Bind with your bias binding. Snuggle!

## Materials

- piece of denim fabric, 30cm (12in) sq.
- scraps of blue, mustard, black and white fabric, at least 5cm (2in) sq.
- piece of chosen fabric for your basket's base, measuring 55 x 22.5cm (11 x 18in/ fat eighth)
- piece of sew-in foam interfacing (such as style-vil smooth foam, Vlieseline), measuring 50cm (20in) sq.
- piece of soft cotton mix, light-weight wadding/batting (such as 279 cotton mix 80/20, Vlieseline), measuring 50cm (20in) sq.
- 4 gold Chicago screws
- scrap piece of leather or faux leather, approx. 15 x 2cm (¾ x 6in) in size
- coordinating threads for topstitching and quilting

## Tools

- your usual sewing needs
- water-soluble marker
- hole punch or bradawl

# Tygkorg Fabric Basket

A basket or two around the house is so handy. This one is made largely from leftover pieces of fabric, so it is a great way to use up scraps that you may already have around your home.

This basket is great for storing all kinds of things, and I guarantee that you will not be able to stop at just one!

**N.B.** *Each panel of the basket is made separately and then the basket is constructed side by side, finishing with the lining. The trick is to not sew right to the end of each panel on the bottom in order to keep the corners sharp. To do this, simply start sewing as normal at the top of the panel and then stop 0.5cm (¼in) from the bottom. Mark this point before you start with your water-soluble marker.*

1   Begin with a piece of wadding about 40 x 30cm (15¾ x 12in) and draw a box on it with your marker, measuring 30 x 22cm (12 x 8¾in). This box represents one of the rectangular sides of the basket, and we are going to 'colour it in' with fabric. On one of the long sides of the rectangle, measure down and mark a 5.5cm (2¼in) line all the way across; this will be the top of the basket. Leave this top rectangle free, as it will be filled with denim at the end.

2   Choose a scrap piece of fabric – mine is approx. 8 x 18cm (3¼ x 7in). Overlapping your drawn edge slightly, sew this scrap onto the wadding/batting by channel quilting multiple vertical lines, each about 1cm (⅜in) apart.

3   Now choose three other fabric scraps and sew them together to make a long piece of three, about the same length as the first fabric piece. Lay this long piece of three face down, right sides together, onto the first piece and sew a regular seam to the right hand side of the rectangular box to attach it. Flip it over and finger press. Channel quilt as you did for the first one. Keep going like this, slightly varying the colours on your box to suit your scraps, and keep quilting vertically. The most important thing is to 'colour in' outside the lines! Make sure that your pieces overlap the lines slightly, as this will ensure there are no gaps. When you have finished colouring the bottom part, redraw the original box lines over the top of the patches. This is helpful for the next step and you can see if you have covered everything.

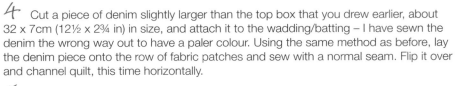

*4* Cut a piece of denim slightly larger than the top box that you drew earlier, about 32 x 7cm (12½ x 2¾ in) in size, and attach it to the wadding/batting – I have sewn the denim the wrong way out to have a paler colour. Using the same method as before, lay the denim piece onto the row of fabric patches and sew with a normal seam. Flip it over and channel quilt, this time horizontally.

*5* Make another rectangular side and two ends of the basket, following the instructions in Steps 1 to 4. Bear in mind that the ends measure 20 x 22cm (7¾ x 8¾in) so you will have to cut two pieces of wadding/batting accordingly. You will also need to measure down and mark a 5.5cm (2¼in) line for the denim top.

*6* The base is 20 x 30cm (7¾ x 12in) and uses the 22.5 x 55cm (11 x 18in/fat eighth) piece of fabric. Simply lay it over the top of a piece of wadding/batting and then quilt it with your desired pattern – I have swapped to a classic diagonal lattice quilt pattern for my base.

*7* Redraw the original rectangular box lines over the top of the coloured patches and attach the panel to a piece of foam interfacing, sewing along the drawn lines. Cut it out, leaving a 0.5cm (¼in) gap outside this sewing line to form a seam allowance. Repeat for the other side and end sections.

*8* Sew the basket sides and ends together, remembering not to sew into the bottom seam. Add the base with the quilted side down. This is your outer.

*9* Make lining from the denim by cutting panels as follows:

**Sides** – 2 pieces, 30 x 22cm (12 x 8¾in)

**Ends** – 2 pieces, 20 x 22cm (7¾ x 8¾in)

**Base** – 1 piece, 20 x 30cm (7¾ x 12in)

Sew these up, taking care not to sew into the bottom seam allowance. Leave a gap in the base of the lining along one side.

10  A bit of squashing is required now. Have the outer the right way out and the lining inside out. Pull the lining on over the outer (the right sides should be together). Sew around the top edge. Turn the box out through the gap in the lining and gently pull everything into place. Push the lining into the box and topstitch the top edge. Close the gap in the lining.

11  Attach a handle to each end of your fabric basket, using your scraps of leather and the Chicago screws. With a hole punch or bradawl make two holes on one end where you want the screws on the basket and make two holes in the handle too. Unscrew the two parts of one Chicago screw and feed it through your punched hole, attaching the handle before screwing it together again. Ensure that your handles are a practical length and that you can use them – mine are about 28cm (11in) long and roughly 5cm (2in) in from either side. In the photo you will see that I have actually used the screws back to front – the flat surface is the 'good side'. I prefer the screw side, but it is really up to you – there is no Chicago screw police!

### Tip
Chicago screws sound exotic but they are easy to find, cheap to buy and actually wonderful for things like this: they are strong and also look really nice.

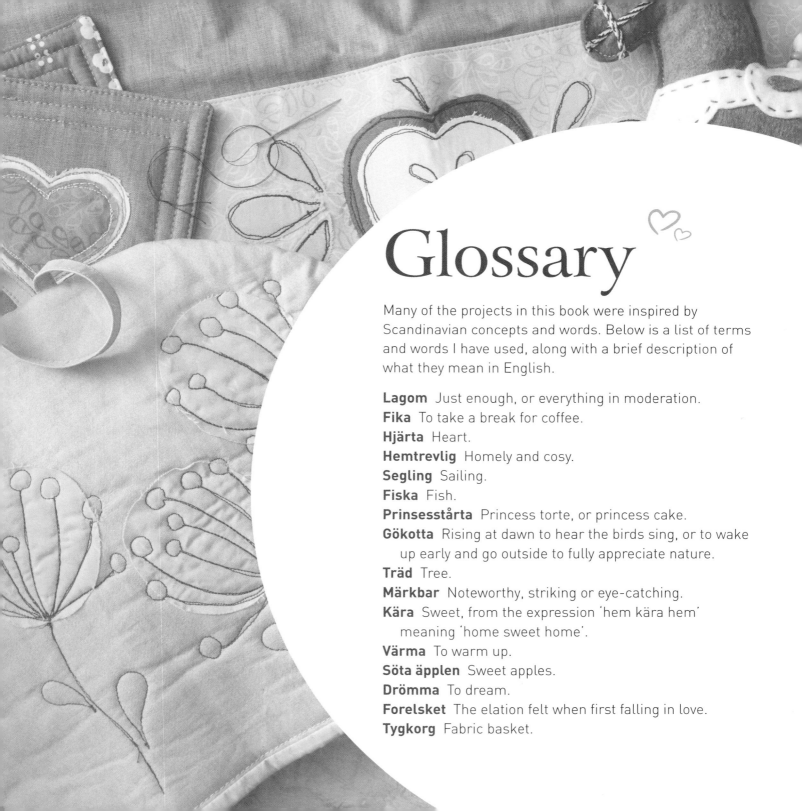

# Glossary

Many of the projects in this book were inspired by Scandinavian concepts and words. Below is a list of terms and words I have used, along with a brief description of what they mean in English.

**Lagom**  Just enough, or everything in moderation.
**Fika**  To take a break for coffee.
**Hjärta**  Heart.
**Hemtrevlig**  Homely and cosy.
**Segling**  Sailing.
**Fiska**  Fish.
**Prinsesstårta**  Princess torte, or princess cake.
**Gökotta**  Rising at dawn to hear the birds sing, or to wake up early and go outside to fully appreciate nature.
**Träd**  Tree.
**Märkbar**  Noteworthy, striking or eye-catching.
**Kära**  Sweet, from the expression 'hem kära hem' meaning 'home sweet home'.
**Värma**  To warm up.
**Söta äpplen**  Sweet apples.
**Drömma**  To dream.
**Forelsket**  The elation felt when first falling in love.
**Tygkorg**  Fabric basket.

# Acknowledgements

This is the bit where my stress levels ratchet up to abnormal as I fret about leaving someone out.

Firstly, my family must get a mention as they are the ones who have been with me every step of the way, cajoling, threatening, coaxing and generally being very good about odd mealtimes, glazed expressions and threads everywhere. The dogs especially have had great forbearance and understanding.

To Pat and Walter Bravo of Art Gallery Fabrics and the team at Hantex, especially Jeanette and Paul in the UK with whom I mostly work; I thank you so much for your generosity. This book would not look as good and it would not even be here were it not for the beauty that is AGF. I love these fabrics so much.

Vlieseline, particularly Sharron, who has been asked to go out to the warehouse armed with scissors more times than I can name ; once again, this book simply wouldn't be here without you. Thank you so much, and also to the other people that I don't even know about who spend time finding me things and then sending them out.

Janome make wonderful machines and I use the lovely Horizon MC 8200 QCP special edition, without which I would not be able to get up in the morning. Just knowing that it is waiting to work with me each day makes it all worthwhile. To Deborah and the team, thank you!

And of course, to my lovely peeps at Search Press: to Katie French and to Emily Adam, to my lovely photographers Paul Bricknell and Stacy Grant, and to Marrianne Miall, Emma Sutcliffe and Juan Hayward in design. Thank you all so very much. Nothing is possible on my own.

**Love Debbie**
Norfolk, 2017